THE OLD AND NEW MAN

The Old and New Man

in the Letters of Paul

BY RUDOLF BULTMANN

TRANSLATED BY KEITH R. CRIM

JOHN KNOX PRESS
Richmond, Virginia

Title of the German original—*Der alte und der neue Mensch in der Theologie des Paulus.* 1964.

English translation published by arrangement with Wissenschaftliche Buchgesellschaft, Darmstadt.

Unless otherwise noted, Scripture quotations are from the *Revised Standard Version of the Bible,* copyrighted 1946 and 1952.

"The Problem of Ethics in the Writings of Paul" first appeared in *Zeitschrift für die neutestamentliche Wissenschaft und die Kunde der älteren Kirche,* No. 23 (1924), pages 123-140; "Romans 7 and Paul's Anthropology," in *Imago dei: Beiträge zur theologischen Anthropologie* (Festschrift for Gustav Krüger), 1932, pages 53-62; and "Adam and Christ in Romans 5," in *Zeitschrift für die neutestamentliche Wissenschaft und die Kunde der älteren Kirche,* No. 50 (1959), pages 145-165.

LIBRARY OF CONGRESS CATALOG CARD NUMBER: 67-24123
GERMAN EDITION © WISSENSCHAFTLICHE BUCHGESELLSCHAFT, DARMSTADT, 1964
ENGLISH TRANSLATION © M. E. BRATCHER, 1967
PRINTED IN THE UNITED STATES OF AMERICA

23-0370

2029

Contents

I

The Problem of Ethics
in the Writings of Paul

In modern Pauline studies the work of Paul Wernle
(*Der Christ und die Sünde bei Paulus,* 1897) is well
known for having pointed out the problem arising from
statements of Paul which, while standing side by side,
seem to contradict each other. There are statements which
say that the one justified is free from sin, has died to sin,
does not live any longer in the flesh but in the Spirit.
Alongside them are others which exhort even the one who
has been justified to fight against sin. The main passages
are Romans 6:1—7:6; 8:1–17; Galatians 5:13–25; and
1 Corinthians 6:9–11. The distinctive nature of the problem is made clear by the fact that the contrasting statements—the indicative and the imperative—are not found
in widely separated parts of the epistles but are very
closely connected. The antinomy they constitute is well
expressed in the paradox of Galatians 5:25, "If we live
by the Spirit, let us also walk by the Spirit."

I

It is characteristic of almost all attempts to solve the
problem[1] that they regard the antinomy as a self-contradiction which must be explained by taking each side—
the indicative and the imperative—separately and ex-

plaining it historically or psychologically by tracing it to specific causes, thus regarding the contradiction itself in historical and psychological terms. No one inquires whether we may here be dealing with a true antinomy, that is, with statements that contradict each other but still belong together, statements that arise out of a common situation and are as a result intimately related.

On the surface it appears that for Paul δικαιοσύνη is an eschatological blessing and that the δικαιωθείς is the new man of the salvation age for whom acting and sinning in this world are no longer possibilities. The indicatives then result from Paul's awareness of eschatology. The imperatives are seen as an inconsistency which was necessary because righteousness, contrary to its proper meaning, is attributed to the man who is still in the world, and this does not fit the eschatological pattern. It was necessary also because of the concept of the will of the holy God who rules over human life in the world. And finally, it was necessary because of the practical need for Paul to suit his message to the needs of the congregation.

In addition, it is possible, in the interest of a psychological understanding, to point to the eschatological tension under which Paul and the early church lived, and to the fact that the meaning or the problematic nature of the life the one justified lives in this world scarcely comes to the attention of one whose gaze is fixed on the end which is about to break in and totally swallow up everything.[2]

Particular reference is made to Paul's conversion experience. In this radical break with the past it is understandable that for Paul sin disappears along with the old life. Finally, appeal may be made to the view of the sacraments in which the sinful nature of man is destroyed through baptism, and also to Christocentric mysticism which holds the view that the new life can be experienced as a present reality. All this indeed serves to elucidate the statement that the one justified is sinless. It also substantiates the view, which is not thought of as a psychological explanation but simply as a fact, that righteousness is an eschatological blessing.

But studies of the problem do not do justice even to this insight, and however much they are correct in some sense, none of them are fully satisfactory. They are not satisfactory because the explanation of the origin of a theory does not explain its meaning. They do not show what the sinlessness of the Christian means for Paul, and to try to interpret his statements historically and psychologically before grasping their meaning is to fail to come to grips with Paul. It results only in giving the statements another meaning.

I would like to demonstrate what I mean by relating it to Weinel's attempt (*Biblische Theologie des N.T.,* 3rd ed., 1921, pp. 316-321) to interpret psychologically the statements about sinlessness. Weinel contends that Paul's theory of sinlessness is based on his experience of the grace of God. On the basis of the grace he has experienced, man *cannot* do anything except the good. Good proceeds from justified man surely and naturally. God's will is the good, love, what is proper and highest for man. For the one who has been justified, a moral life is merely the necessary activity performed by a religiously filled inner life in order to express itself as life (p. 370). Our suspicion is already aroused by the interpretation of the imperatives as a relapse into legalism (p. 322), since in Paul imperatives and indicatives so obviously belong together (Rom. 6 and the other passages cited above). It is also clear that Paul is by no means saying that the one justified is unable to act in any other way; in the decisive passages he says he *can* act differently (e.g., Rom. 8:12; Gal. 5:25). Above all it is clear that Paul does not think that sinlessness consists of enthusiasm, will, and power for performing the good, but rather that it is something negative, freedom from the power of sin. It is also clear that Paul regards the one justified as an eschatological entity, a miraculous being, and not as a man whose proper, highest nature is to be developed. So Weinel makes Paul say something quite different from what he really says, or at the very least he does not take Paul's statements seriously because their real meaning seems to him absurd.

It seems to me that Wernle himself betrays the error of this method of interpretation when (p. 105) quite apart from the psychological interpretation he tries to find the basis of the theory of sinlessness in the logic of the subject matter itself. This is what is meant when this theory is termed "purely and severely doctrinaire"; it is the consequence of the teaching of justification by faith. "If faith alone saves us and judgment spares all who believe, then the ethical nature of religion can be preserved only by postulating that justification merges with re-birth." This explanation is not possible either, because it presupposes that justification is conceivable in itself without doing away with sin. But can justification have any meaning for Paul if it is not primarily freedom from sin? In no case can it mean that it is the remission of the sins committed prior to baptism, but has no significance for the subsequent life of the one justified. This would fail to recognize its eschatological character, that it is the *eschaton,* the definitive event. In that case sinlessness would have to be taken as a postulate, with the result that the imperatives directly contradict the indicatives, and alongside an ethic of miracle there now appears an ethic of will (p. 89). This seems to me to be the primary mistake of this interpretation, since Paul bases the imperatives on the fact of justification, deriving them from the indicatives. It is because the Christian is free from sin through justification that he must fight against sin. "If we live by the Spirit, let us also walk by the Spirit."

II

If we are to understand Paul's paradox we must call attention also to a second error of this method of interpretation, which has already been mentioned. It is contained in Wernle's statement that the indicatives are an *ethic* of the miraculous. The fact is that in Paul's statements about the sinlessness of the one justified it is not a matter of ethics at all. All those interpretations are unconsciously based on a specific understanding of man, in particular of justified man, which is very different from Paul's. Even though Paul's understanding may seem absurd it must still be taken seriously in interpretation. In all those attempts, the sinlessness of man is conceivable only as his moral ability, or as his spiritual condition, that is, as the possibility or the drive to achieve the good, to act perfectly. It is only in this way that Paul's theory of sinlessness can be termed "idealism that storms heaven" (Holtzmann, *Lehrbuch der neutestamentlichen Theologie,* II, 2nd ed., p. 164), or the "formula of an ethically idealistic optimism" (Lietzmann, *Handbuch zum N.T.,* III, 2nd ed., p. 66 on Rom. 6:14). Only in this way is it conceivable that Holtzmann (pp. 166f) could speak in reference to Paul's statements of the "irreconcileable co-existence of a strictly supernatural, mystical theory having a 'critical act of atonement' and of an empirical, psychological concept in which a sudden destruction is turned into a gradual disappearance of sin." Or that Lietzmann (p. 63 on Rom. 6:4) could say more cautiously that Paul probably came to accept some sort of developmental theory. This contradicts Paul's view that the righteousness of the one justified is a δικαιοσύνη (ἐκ) θεοῦ. And above all it contradicts the Pauline concept of the justified man who stands entirely on faith. In contrast to the way Paul regards man, the basis of this theory is the concept of man and his possibilities dominant in both ancient and modern rationalism and idealism, namely, the concept that man is able to achieve the good. But it is clear that for Paul there does not exist any concept of the good which determines conduct and which is to be realized through conduct. Consequently, his concept of the justi-fied man has nothing in common with the ideal of man based on such a view. That view of necessity transforms sinlessness into a realizable ideal, while in Paul's writings righteousness, or sinlessness, is eschatological and miracu-lous in character. It is the already realized mode of existence of the one justified. If the imperatives are rele-vant to this mode of existence they certainly cannot be the way of achieving it. Consequently Wernle totally distorts the matter when he surrenders his earlier insight, ex-pressed in the discussion of Windisch's book (*Theologische Literaturzeitung,* No. 34, 1909, col. 588), and describes sinlessness not as a necessity but as a possibility after repentance, and holds that in the last analysis the de-scriptive indicatives are simply intensified imperatives.

III

Before I attempt to explain Paul's concept of the nature of redeemed man in such a way as to make the imperatives and the whole paradox or antinomy intelligible, I want to look at one other attempt to solve the problem in another manner. This attempt was earlier than the ones discussed above and is vastly superior to them because of the profound way in which it deals with the question. I am referring to the position of F. C. Baur, which I will sketch here on the basis of his posthumous lectures on New Testament theology (ed. F. F. Baur, 1864). He makes no attempt to interpret the contradiction in historical or psychological terms by tracing each side back to a different starting point, but rather tries to grasp them as arising from the real content of the doctrine of justification (pp. 174-182).

According to Baur, in justification man's will receives a new principle, the "principle of fulfillment of the law or of moral behavior." As a result, it is no contradiction for Paul to "depict the ethical demand in regard to sin, the duty to die to sin, as actually already being dead to it, and at the same time, as a matter of great urgency." The indicatives express the fact that the new principle has been received into the will. Since, however, we are dealing with a principle of the will, it is natural to express this in imperatives. The believer is really justified because "in the Spirit, as the principle which truly is at work in him, he has been placed in the relationship to God which corresponds to the ethical ideal." Mere quantitative fulfillment of the law is now replaced by a qualitative, the value of which is determined by the person's attitude. The one justified is therefore by no means ungodly, and the contrast of faith and works has become a relative one. Indeed, even in the period of the Old Testament works could be the product of a proper attitude, and, conversely, faith, as a vital attitude, can naturally not fail to produce works.

The questions raised here are relevant in that the antinomy is seen in terms of the nature of the problem. But the answer is false because it is stated in terms of an idealistic concept of the nature of man. The more clearly the answer is stated, the more clearly we see that the picture of man given here is very different from that held by Paul. For Paul, man stands before God as a sinner, and justification does not consist of an attitude, a moral desire. To accept this would be to deny the eschatological character of justification, to deny that justification is God's miraculous act, or God's incomprehensible judgment. This is the same problem discussed in section II.

Juncker (*Die Ethik des Apostels Paulus,* I, 1904) treats the problem in similar fashion, but he does not come close to Baur's dialectic, or seem to be aware of its consequences. Still I wish to discuss him in this connection in order to attempt to gain gradually, by this critical method, a correct picture of Paul's view. According to Juncker (pp. 127ff), justification is also man's moral renewal. The faith on which it rests is the decisive moral act which produces an immeasurable line of other acts, indeed a whole, unified life. But if faith is really the decisive moral act (and this is impossible according to Romans 10), then the decision is placed in man's hands, justification is dependent on his act, and man is not radically conceived of as a sinner. How could a sinner come to have faith, if this is the decisive act? It is apparent that in Juncker's presentation man really saves himself (pp.

150f), for he says that the human spirit is related to God, and when man acts by the power of the divine Spirit he is really acting on the basis of his own being, his "natural" tendency. "God's Spirit is wedded to man's spirit, and a fully new spiritual life is the fruit of this intimate relationship" (p. 143). This does not in the least correspond to the way Paul sees man.

The much debated question (cf. Juncker, pp. 42ff) of whether Adam's fall can be traced to the flesh, which is originally and essentially conditioned by sin, or whether the flesh became sinful only as a consequence of the fall—that is to say, in Juncker's terms, whether the connection between flesh and sin is only an empirical one that has come about during the course of history—can be made clear in terms of the case itself. The question is meaningless. That is, it is irrelevant for Paul's total view, whatever speculations he may have made about the question. The question of *iustitia originalis* was of primary significance for the scholastics and for Luther because it was decisive for their concept of sin and consequently for their concept of redemption. It was the question of whether sin was the loss of the *donum superadditum* or the total corruption of human nature, and whether redemption could somehow be achieved by man or was totally dependent on God. For Paul the question of man's condition had not yet been put in terms of this problem: it was a question of whether the man with whom he was dealing was sinful. Whether there had once been a man (Adam) for whom this was not the case, and to whom other possibilities for life were open—even if Paul had developed this thought—was a superfluous speculation which had nothing to say about the man who is the object of justification. For this man there is no possibility open except to be a sinner. For this man a positive relation to God exists only on the basis of the divine grace and not on the basis of some natural endowment. This is evident in Paul's view of the meaning of the law for salvation history—that it brings man into the situation where it is clear that there is no possible road to God except that of grace (Rom. 5:20f; 7:7–25; Gal. 3:19, 22). Any such speculation must be left entirely out of account where it is a matter of man as he is and as he comes to be justified.

Romans 7:14–25 should not deceive anyone into thinking that here the inner man or the mind is a part of man that is not characterized by sin. In the sentence in verse 18, "For I know that nothing good dwells within me, that is, in my flesh," the words "that is" do not introduce an illustration but a correction. The flesh and the inner man are not two equally real elements in man. Paul is expressing as strongly as possible in unequivocal dualistic terminology that man is actually determined only by sin. And the statements about mind and inner man express the fact that sin is sin, not fate or natural destiny, and that it is a part of man's nature to be under God's claims. Romans 7:7ff does not contain Paul's confessions, or a description of the spiritual state of unredeemed man, but the presentation of the objective nature of unredeemed man from the viewpoint of the one who is redeemed.[3] We can say paradoxically that the inner man is something that is not real for man in the same way that flesh and sin are real.

IV

Let us now attempt to understand the antinomy, the existence of indicatives and imperatives side by side, in terms of the material itself; in other words, attempt to understand the phenomenon of the δικαιωθείς. It will be in the interests of clarity to make one more detour and call attention to analogous phenomena, the first of which is characteristic of stoic ethics, a feature, in the aspect we are discussing here, very close to Baur's position.

Just as the sinner (ἁμαρτωλός) and the just man (δίκαιος) are contrasted in Paul's thought, in Stoicism the simple man (φαῦλος) is contrasted to the wise (σοφός) or mature (τέλειος). The contrast is radical. The simple man has no virtue at all, while the mature man has all virtue. Virtue is indeed indivisible, and whoever has virtue has all virtue. There cannot be any development, any transition from simple to mature. It is a well-known fact that in the middle period of Stoicism this radical position was moderated to the extent of inserting the concept of striver (προκόπτων) between the simple man and the mature. The striver is a man who is moving toward maturity. He is neither simple nor mature, or to say it better, he is both, yet in such a way that his being is determined by maturity. This maturity lies beyond the striver as an idea toward which he continually moves. As a result, the apparently contradictory statements—indicative and imperative—can be made in reference to the striver in the same way as to the man who has been justified as interpreted by Baur.

Clearly the phenomenon of the striver contains a formal analogy to justified man in Paul's writings. It is only a formal one, but it can sharpen our senses for understanding the distinctive nature of Paul's position. To consider only one point: maturity does not correspond to righteousness, because it describes the general norm of human behavior, while the concept of righteousness is not characterized by the idea of a universal norm of human existence but by the position of the individual, concrete person in the sight of God. The goal or benefit of righteousness is not the achievement of an ideal of human existence, but freedom from our very concrete sin in the sight of God. It is based on a totally irrational view of human nature in which it is not a question of an idea of man, but of individual, concrete men.

It is natural to expect that genuine analogies to Paul's position would exist in the histories of other religions, above all, those in which the believer seeks in the present age to lay hold of an otherworldly salvation that always remains an *eschaton;* that is, in cases where a problem is caused by the continuation of earthly life in a manner similar to the problem we find in Paul's letters. It is appropriate for more than one reason to compare Paul with the Hellenistic mystery religions and with Hellenistic mysticism. Such analogies may bring us still closer to an understanding of Paul.

In the sphere of Hellenism with which we are dealing the contrast between those born again and those not born again corresponds to the contrast between the sinner and the just man. I have chosen this terminology in the interest of conciseness because it represents the facts fairly, even though its usage is restricted. The nature of the one born again is truly self-contradictory because he is not that which he appears to be, inasmuch as that which he is does not appear. This contradiction between the otherworldly nature of the one born again and his empirical existence is expressed in the *Corpus Hermeticum,* Chap. XIII, p. 3, as follows:

> "Seeing in myself an immaterial vision, produced by the mercy of God, I have left myself in order to enter into

an immortal body, and I am now no longer what I was, but I have been begotten in the intellect. This cannot be taught, and it cannot be seen by means of the material elements through which we see below. This is why I am no longer concerned with this initial created form which was my own. I have no more color, cannot be touched, and do not extend in space; all that is foreign to me. Now, my child, you see me with your eyes, but what I am you cannot understand when you look at me with your body's eyes and with the physical sight. It is not with those eyes that anyone can see me now, my child."

This point of view is also the basis of the portrait of John in the accounts of the apocryphal Acts of John. The Apostle says of his portrait, "The picture resembles me, and yet not me, my child, but the picture of my body." The true picture of the Apostle would have to be painted with other colors, such as faith and knowledge, with those attributes which constitute the otherworldly nature of the one born again.

The other world which is meant here is not an idea that will be realized in the future, but is really present and thought of as being natural, substantial, as is expressed in characteristic fashion in this logically thought out presentation of the heavenly or spiritual body.[4] Man is related to the other world by participation in it. Something in him has come from that other world, that world of light. Depending on which mythical or cultic tradition determines the thought patterns, it is there from the very beginning as a primeval portion of light that has descended into matter, or it is the result of some change or influx due to a sacrament or an ecstatic experience. This something in man is regarded as the essential element in the one born again. And yet it has no necessary connection with the empirical man, with his acts and his fate. This basic point of view finds expression in the most varied forms, above all in the statements that consecration, or *gnosis,* liberates man from fate (εἱμαρμένη). The devotee of Isis speaks (*Metamorphoses of Apuleius,* Chap. XI, p. 15):

> "Let fortune go and fume in another place; let her find some other object for her cruelty; for fortune has no power over those who have devoted their lives to serve and honor the majesty of our goddess . . . let such as are not devoted to her see and admit their error: 'Behold here is Lucius who is delivered from misery by the providence of the goddess Isis and rejoices therefore and triumphs in victory over his fortune.' "

It is similar in the case of *gnosis* (*Corpus Hermeticum,* Chap. XII, p. 9):

> "You will find, my child, that the intellect, that is, the self of God, in reality dominates all these things. It dominates fate, law, and all the rest. And nothing is impossible for it, neither the establishing of the human soul superior to fate, nor, if it has been negligent, perhaps subjugating it to fate."

Particularly characteristic is the Hermetic teaching that has come down from Zosimos (Reitzenstein, *Poimandres,* p. 103; and *Hellenistische-Mysterienreligion,* p. 152):

> The pneumatic man, as the one who knows himself, must not put anything in order by magic, even if he considers it good, nor must he force Necessity, but rather act according to nature and judgment. Seeking only himself and having known God, let him hold fast the nameless triad, and let fate do what it wishes to do with his clay, that is, the body.[5]

We might say that man's concrete existence is no longer relevant; it does not concern the man born again, the pneumatic man, and so is to be ignored. The practical consequence of this can be either libertinism or asceticism. The one born again is really not the concrete man at all, but something within the concrete man. The continuity between the one born again and the old man is destroyed and consequently the one born again has lost any definite, individual character. The other world which he can experience in ecstasy, for example, is a common "life"; in ecstasy all individual being is extinguished. It is not possible to speak of forgiveness of sins here; forgiveness is not something general like "life." It would mean that the concept of the other world is determined by a relationship to the concrete individual whose sin is forgiven.

V

Even though some difference is indicated here, we cannot help seeing that there is an extensive relationship between Paul's thought and Hellenistic mysticism. It is not only that in Paul also the result of salvation is called "life." That in itself might only indicate an influence of terminology. It is rather that for Paul justification is based on a sacramental act—baptism. Moreover, Paul regards the spirit that is given at baptism as a supernatural but substantial power which then dwells within man (cf. Rom. 5:5; 8:11, 16; 2 Cor. 2:10–16, etc.). Paul's view of flesh-spirit possesses to a considerable degree the character of the metaphysical dualism that is typical of Hellenistic mystery religions. That is to say, flesh and spirit are thought of as natural or substantial powers, as is seen with particular clarity in the doctrine of the resurrection with its idea of the spiritual body.

Such passages as Romans 8:15, 26 and Galatians 4:6 and especially 1 Corinthians 14 and 2 Corinthians 12:1–4 show that Paul saw the composition of the other world in ecstatic experiences. It is clear that in speaking of Paul we must take account of specifically mystical ecstasy, which is to be distinguished from prophetic ecstasy not as a psychic occurrence, but with respect to its significance.

For the prophet (as for shamans in primitive religions, *mutatis mutandis*) ecstasy is a means for carrying out his task. That is, in the ecstatic experience he receives the word of God which he is to proclaim, as in primitive religions ecstasy is the means for gaining or increasing magical powers for purposes such as soothsaying. On the other hand, for the mystic ecstasy is an end in itself. The words which he hears in ecstasy are meant for him alone, and for others they are "things that cannot be told," as Paul himself says in 2 Corinthians 12:4. Finally, it cannot be denied that in Paul's letters ascetic themes are derived from that dualism and that mystic concept of the other world. They can be clearly seen in both the motivation of the warning against unchastity (1 Cor. 6:12–20) and the discussion of marriage (1 Cor. 7), along with other themes.

On this basis then, it is possible to arrive at an understanding of the antinomy—the occurrence of indicatives and imperatives side by side—that can claim to grasp it in terms of the material itself. For the mystic, otherworldly salvation is a present reality, and since this is the case the indicatives can be used in a natural way to speak of that salvation. The imperatives do not really conflict with this, since they express the fact that the empirical, concrete human being is to be canceled out. If it is necessary to speak of a contradiction, it is to be found in the basic concept of mystical piety.

In this view there is no need to be disturbed by the fact that Paul uses the totally unmystical terms "righteousness" and "to be justified" as the distinctive expressions for describing his idea of salvation. These occur from time to time in Hellenistic mysticism (*Corpus Hermeticus,* Chap. XIII, p. 9), and they may also have mystical significance in Paul (Rom. 6:7?; 8:30?; 1 Cor. 1:30?; 6:11).[6] Much more serious is the objection that Paul develops so little those approaches to asceticism which in mysticism are the characteristic expression of the canceling out of concrete man. But quite apart from this objection, the hypothetical construction breaks down.

VI

It is impossible to overlook the fundamental difference between Paul's view and comparable phenomena in other systems of thought. Indeed, it has already been indicated above. For Paul, justification, deliverance from sin, is an eschatological benefit. Its otherworldly character is different from that of the "idea" in Stoicism, and from that of the "supernatural" in Hellenistic mysticism. It is an event, an occurrence which results from God's action and constitutes God's judgment. This corresponds to the fact that Paul does not regard God as a metaphysical entity which can be described in terms of its attributes such as light, life, immortality, etc., as in the Hellenistic realm. No, God is active will. When Paul proclaims God's grace he is not proclaiming a previously unknown or unhonored attribute of God; that is, a new, purified concept of God. He is speaking of God's new, saving act. This says to us that Paul thinks of the other world in terms of its relationship to the individual, concrete man. Naturally this is not to be taken in terms of modern individualism. Paul is speaking of mankind.[7] But not even this idea of mankind is determined by the idea of *man;* it is determined by the concept of individual, concrete men, *with whom God is dealing.* It is only insofar as God is dealing with men that it is possible (in the Pauline sense) to speak of God. As a result, the relationship of man to the other world is not one of endless progress or of participation, but it is characterized by faith. This faith is man's obedience in submission to God's saving deed and in renunciation of any claim to be able to establish on his own terms his relationship to God. It is the belief that only through God's judgment is man justified.[8] Righteousness, or sinlessness, is then—paradoxically—not a change in man's moral quality. It is neither something that can be detected in man nor something he can experience in the mystical sense; it is something that can only be believed in.[9] Of course Paul experienced ecstasy, but for him it is a special charism and not the specifically Christian mode of life (cf. 1 Cor. 12–14).

By an extension of what Paul says explicitly it is possible to say even that sin itself is not something that can be perceived in the empirical man, but that it exists only insofar as man is seen from the viewpoint of God. It is therefore not identical with moral errors, however much it may express itself in them. In terms of the Christian position it cannot be perceived before the moment when it is forgiven. This interpretation is derived from the correct interpretation of Romans 7:7–25, where the situation of unredeemed man is depicted as it appears in retrospect to the one redeemed (see above, p. 16). This also results from the fact that according to Paul the law prepares man for grace by leading him into sin. If man has a positive relationship to God only when he knows God's grace, that is, when he knows that he is a sinner, then in the strict sense he can know that he is a sinner in God's sight only if he knows God's grace. As a consequence, it can be said in terms of Paul's basic concept of justification that sin is not something that can be perceived empirically. And the same holds true for righteousness. This means that the identity of the one justified with the empirical man is something that is *believed.*

It is the concrete, empirical man (who from God's viewpoint is a sinner) who is justified, whose sins are forgiven. Consequently, the relationship of the one justified to the other world is not something that exists apart from or alongside his concrete actions and fate. The concrete man who acts and suffers is also the one who is justified, and his actions and his fate have now (from the viewpoint of God, or from that of faith) taken on a new significance. Here the difference between Paul and Hellenistic mysticism is obvious. It appears most clearly in the statements in 2 Corinthians 4:7–11. Can we say that Paul's empirical fate does not concern him any longer? On the contrary, it served the function "that the life of Jesus may be manifested in our mortal flesh." To speak here of "Christ mysticism" strikes me as totally erroneous; it is in concrete fate itself that—from the point of view of faith—the otherworldly life of Jesus is revealed, not in the *feelings* of the one who suffers. Indeed, from the point of view of faith it is a paradoxical reversal of values, because we are not dealing with various experiences which as such mediate power from the other world.

The same approach is also expressed in the statements which say the body and its members are in the service of

God (cf. Rom. 6:12–19; 12:1; 1 Cor. 6:19). These passages do not prove "that the apostle regarded man's mental and material makeup as open to spiritual influence" and that therefore the relationship of flesh to sin is only an empirical one, as Juncker thought (p. 46). All these passages are speaking about the one justified, whose fleshly, sinful life has been ended. What they say can be said only of the one who has been justified. They show that he is a totally concrete man, and that his empirical existence, his activities, are determined by the fact that he has been justified. As a result, the continuity between the old man and the new is not disrupted as it is in Hellenistic mysticism. The one justified is the concrete man who bears the burden of his past, his present, and his future, and who also is subject to the moral imperatives. These imperatives do not disappear, but take on the new meaning of obedience to God.

The moral actions of the new man can naturally not have the significance of "works" any longer; that is, they cannot become the basis of man's relation to the other world or be the means of achieving righteousness, because it has already been bestowed. They can only have the function of obedience. The whole man knows he is standing before God, and insofar as he acts he places himself at God's disposal (Rom. 6:13 "yield yourselves to God"). But in his destiny he cannot achieve or experience anything which an unbeliever cannot objectively achieve or experience (the meaning of the actions is seen only by faith); neither is anything special demanded of him in his obedience that is not also demanded of others. The moral demands have no new content for him, and his moral behavior is different from that of others only in that it is now behavior in obedience.[10] God demands of the one justified only what is good, well-pleasing, and perfect, what is virtuous and worthy of praise (Rom. 12:2; Phil. 4:8). The moral commandments of the Old Testament are just as valid as the catalogs of virtues and vices in the practical tradition of Hellenistic Judaism. Paul says explicitly that the demands of the law are to be affirmed (Rom. 7:12, 14) and that the conduct of the one justified is the fulfillment of the law (Rom. 13:8–10; Gal. 5:14).

The negative side, the disappearance of the ceremonial demands of the law, is not the result of justification by faith any more than a new moral law is to be derived from justification (or from faith). The result is only that the demands are not to be fulfilled any longer as "works." Moreover, from the standpoint of faith it is of no avail, it is nothing (Gal. 5:6; 6:15; 1 Cor. 7:19); that is to say, ceremonial demands are in themselves of no significance. Paul opposes them as "works." If they are eliminated as works, then they naturally will disappear wherever they are not reasonable demands that grow out of his concrete situation. In other words, they do not disappear because of a specific moral ideal which is valid for those who have been justified, but simply because of a moral insight which is available to all.

If the one justified must place his body at God's disposal, and if this has consequences for his moral behavior, do we then have to say that he can be distinguished from the unbeliever in some generally perceptible manner? Is it not also Paul's opinion that the life of the believer is clearly different from his former conduct and from that of his heathen environment? (Cf. Rom. 6:12–23; 1 Cor. 6:9–11; Phil. 2:15, etc.) Above all he sees the spirit which the believer possesses as the power for a new moral life (cf. Rom. 8:4–14; Gal. 5:16–25, etc.). Even so it would be an oversimplification to say that the real nature of those justified can be observed in their moral behavior. The decisive element, the righteousness which results only from God's verdict, cannot be perceived except through the eyes of faith. (In the same way the state of the unbeliever as a state of sin is perceived only through faith.)

Of course the new behavior itself can be perceived by anyone. It is also obvious that the moral demands take on a new seriousness as that which God commands the one who really acts in obedience to him, and therefore his behavior is actually new. The crucial point, however, is that all human moral wholeness means nothing without God's decisive verdict. Righteousness depends only on that and not on moral deeds. Consequently, righteousness is not openly perceptible because moral behavior is possible without it. Under certain circumstances the heathen also do what the law requires (Rom. 2:14). Therefore, without God's decisive verdict even the best moral behavior is meaningless. Whether or not it really is obedience is something that cannot be openly perceived.

This doctrine can be so formulated that the believer never ceases to be ungodly, and is always justified as ungodly, even though this conclusion cannot be clearly drawn on the basis of Romans 4:5: "And to one who does not work but trusts him who justifies the ungodly, his faith is reckoned as righteousness." We must comment here that Paul did not follow this thought to its conclusion. For him the concepts "faith" and "having faith" almost always keep (under the influence of the traditional missionary terminology) something of the sense of initial confession, of first coming to the faith, even though in the case of "faith" in contrast to "works" this meaning has almost disappeared. Because Paul expected the end of the present aeon to come soon, the life of the believer in this world did not become a problem for him in the same way it did for Luther. Paul does not say that faith daily conquers sin any more than he says we must repent every day and continually receive new forgiveness. Wernle, however, seeks to understand Paul's proclamation in terms of its being limited to that period because it was missionary theology. He says, "If Paul had carried this concept through [the doctrine of justification by grace alone without works] his theology would have come immeasurably closer to that of the Reformers, for how can a man who has passed this verdict on himself in the sight of God ever cease to feel that he is a sinner who needs God's grace?" (p. 96). It seems to me, however, that the main task of interpretation is not to show how a particular concept is limited in its expression by the situation of that age, but rather to develop the concept in all its consequences and in this way make its uniqueness easily recognizable.[11] But then we must say that if we take seriously the thought that man can stand before God as just only on the basis of grace, then he is always justified as an ungodly man. Otherwise God's grace would no longer have the significance of grace for him.

But as the whole being of the one justified is determined by grace, so are also the imperatives to which he is subject; because this subjection belongs to the mode of existence of the one justified. The believer can understand this existence only as God's gift. Just as the ethical demands expressed in the imperatives are God's commands for him, so the attitude of obedience which corresponds to the demands is God's gift, given by the Spirit, but in such a way that the demands do not lose their nature as imperatives. The paradox is thus fully understandable in faith: "If we live by the Spirit, let us also walk by the Spirit."

1. In addition to Wernle's work the problem is discussed in a monograph by Windish, "Taufe und Sünde im ältesten Christentum bis auf Origines" (1908). See also various discussions of Pauline theology or of early Christian thought.

2. In contrast to this, we should not stress too strongly the fact that the view of the approaching end also serves Paul as motivation for an ethical appeal (e.g., Rom. 13:11–14; 1 Thess. 5:1–10) even though, strictly speaking, this contradicts the fact that the eschatological tension motivated the indicatives and let the imperatives be forgotten. This inconsistency can be tolerated.

3. Cf. Wilhelm Heitmüller, *Zeitschrift für Theologie und Kirche*, No. 27 (1917), pp. 139f.

4. Cf. Richard Reitzenstein, *Hellenistische-Mysterienreligion*, 2nd ed., pp. 121-124, 135. Also *Corpus Hermeticum*, Chap. XIII, pp. 3, 14.

5. See also Reitzenstein, *op. cit.*, pp. 151-156; and Anrich, *Das antike Mysterienwesen*, pp. 90-92.

6. Cf. Reitzenstein, *op. cit.*, pp. 112-116.

7. Without, of course, the abstract concept "mankind."

8. The various nuances in the usage of the concept of "faith" are not important here. In my estimation they are essentially the result of Paul's adapting to the vocabulary of the Hellenistic Christian communities, or to that of Christian missionary effort.

9. We should abandon the old quarrel whether the δικαιωθείς is only *regarded* by God as righteous, or whether he also *is* righteous. Naturally, in Paul's meaning, the one whom God regards as just *is* just. Cf. especially Romans 5:19: "For as by one man's disobedience many were made sinners, so by one man's obedience many will be made righteous." In the same way that sinners, as a result of Adam's sin, really *are* sinners, and not merely regarded as such, so the righteous really *are* righteous. Cf. 2 Corinthians 5:21. The quarrel could arise only because δικαιωθείς was interpreted in an idealistic sense as the ethical condition or attitude of man. It has been shown above that this is false. In this sense he is also not regarded as such by God.

10. This statement is dealing only with basic ideas and leaves the previously mentioned ascetic elements out of consideration.

11. I would certainly not presume to suppose that by this attempt to understand a specific part of Paul's thought I had

succeeded in grasping the whole Paul as a historical phenomenon. My observations are not directed against Heitmüller's thesis (*Luthers Stellung in der Religionsgeschichte des Christentums,* 1917, p. 21) "that in many respects Paul is not so much the father of the Reformation as he is the father of the ancient and the medieval church." I would merely like to direct attention to the words "in many respects"; I attach more importance to Luther's relationship to Paul than Heitmüller does. Neither do I share the view, which as far as I know was first put forward by Wrede, that for Paul the doctrine of justification had merely an apologetic and polemical significance in his missionary work. I believe on the contrary that it was central for his whole position. Still, I am concerned here only with the meaning of the doctrine, and the practical circumstances which led Paul to develop this doctrine do not affect its meaning.

II

Romans 7
and Paul's Anthropology

The much discussed problem of Romans 7 is usually
stated in terms of the question: who is the "I" who is
speaking? Is it the man under the law, or is it the believer?
And if it is the one subject to the law is it man under the
law in general, or is it Paul speaking specifically of his
own development? It seems to me that these questions have
been adequately discussed and that there can be no doubt
about the answer. It is the situation of the man under the
law in general that is described here, and described as seen
by the eyes of the one freed from the law by Christ. The
most recent monograph I know of that discusses the
question, that of W. G. Kümmel, treated the problems
with exemplary caution and came to correct conclusions.[1]

It seems to me, however, that in the previous discussions a further problem has not been adequately dealt
with. In what does the divided state of existence under
the law as described in Romans 7:14ff consist? According
to verses 15–20 it consists in the fact that the desire to do
good is always destroyed by doing evil. It is customary to
say that man would like to fulfill the law because it is
God's good and holy will (v. 12), but he does not fulfill
it and never gets beyond good intentions. In this view the
θέλειν (vv. 15–28) has as its object the commandments of the law. The practically executed κατεργάζεσθαι

(vv. 15–20), ποιεῖν (vv. 15–21), and πράσσειν (vv. 15, 19) are then the violations of the commandments. The συνφάναι (v. 16) and the συνήδεσθαι (v. 22) are the consent to the demands of the law, to the commandments. Man then is torn between the two because the sin which expresses itself in covetousness (v. 7) constantly overcomes his good intentions. There seems to be a parallel in Ovid's *Metamorphoses,* Chap. VII, pp. 20f: "video meliora proboque, deteriora sequor."[2] Is this interpretation tenable?

In order to carry out this interpretation is it not necessary to weaken the practicing of evil to merely an incomplete, inconsistent fulfilling of the law, when really the words are intended to express a totally and basically perverted behavior? Can Paul overlook the fact that in many cases the Jew fulfills the law as he testifies he himself did in Philippians 3:6: "as to righteousness under the law blameless." Romans 7 is not Paul's confessions but a description of Jewish existence in general. Because this is so it must therefore also be applicable to Paul's life as a Jew. But is this the case if the conflict described is really between the acceptance of the demands of the law by the will and their rejection in deeds?

The main difficulty is that what this view would regard here as the sinful nature of the Jews is not such in the rest of Paul's writings, and what is elsewhere regarded as the real sin of the Jews would not even enter the picture here!

It is self-evident that for Paul transgression of the law is sin. The Jews as well as the heathen commit this sin (Rom. 3:19). The real guilt of the Jews is not only the self-contradiction (Rom. 2:17–24) that because of their transgressions they are guilty in God's sight and at the same time claim to rely on the law, so that "the renunciation with which Paul entered into faith" was "simply his coming to regret this situation."[3] That would only result in the law's remaining in force and justification through Christ would come to the one who earnestly listened to the law, and seeing his sins, truly regretted them.

But the antithesis of faith and works of law takes us beyond this. Paul's "regret" (in this connection he significantly never speaks of regret) does not consist in the fact that as a believer he recognizes his former transgressions, but that he condemns his earlier zeal for the law and his fulfillment of the law (Phil. 3:4ff) in the same manner as he brings against the Jews the basic reproach not that they transgress the law, but that they are zealous for the law (Rom. 10:2f). Because they think they are superior to the heathen in God's sight Paul must bring to their attention the fact that because they are transgressors of the law they are no better than the heathen (Rom. 2:17–24). Paul nowhere argues against observation of the law on the ground that it leads to despair, and nowhere does he praise faith as the way out of the conflict that is caused by our consciences. His basic objection to observing the law is not that transgressions make it a false path which never reaches the goal (that is in effect the concept of 4 Esdras).[4] Rather he argues that the path leads in the wrong direction because its meaning lies in its claim to lead to "their own righteousness" (Rom. 10:3; Phil. 3:9). It is not evil works, violations of the law, that make the Jews unacceptable to God; their intention to become right with God by keeping the law is the sin that is brought to light by their transgressions. The divine purpose of the law is to bring this sin to light, so that the true nature of sin may be seen (Rom. 5:20f; Gal. 3:19; 21–24; cf. Rom. 4:13–16). The knowledge of sin which comes through the law (Rom. 3:20) consists in the fact that the law leads man into concrete sin; this shows that man sins because he is a sinner. The opposite is not true—that he becomes a sinner only because he sins. This is the clear meaning of Romans 7:7–13, as will soon become apparent.

But what is the real sin of the Jews? What does the perversity of the law consist in? As soon as Paul has presented for the first time the doctrine of the righteousness of God on the basis of faith apart from law (Rom. 3:21–26) the next question is: what then becomes of our boasting (v. 27)? The boasting, the putting confidence in the flesh (Phil. 3:3f), characterizes the Jewish attitude under the law in that the Jew makes the law and its demands for obedience into the occasion for boasting. So faith is not (as in Jewish usage) the trust in God's gracious forgiveness which produces contrition and which leads the sinner back to the path which he deserted when he transgressed the law. And the action of the will contained in faith is not the attitude of contrition and penance characteristic of Jewish piety, which turns away from the transgressions, but it is obedience; that is, it is primarily submission to the new way of salvation, to God's grace, and the renouncing of one's own righteousness, the turning away from the path of works. It is not the self-condemnation of the old life as a life stained by transgressions, a condemnation that could be and was pronounced in and on the existence under the law (4 Esdras), but it is the sacrifice of that which was, from the point of view of the law, a source of pride or gain (Phil. 3:7–9), of that which the old existence affirmed. This corresponds to the fact that for the uncircumcized believer the law was no longer binding, so that to adopt it was to fall back into the life of flesh (Gal. 3:3).

I am convinced it is impossible that in Romans 7:14ff this basic idea, this characteristically Pauline idea, could have been abandoned in favor of the trite thought "video meliora proboque, deteriora sequor." I believe however that I can quite easily show that the sense of Romans 7:14ff is entirely different; I can do it quite easily as soon as we recognize that the anthropology presupposed in this interpretation is not Paul's.

This anthropology, which I shall simply call subjective, presupposes that the "wanting" of which Paul is speaking is the intention which always fulfills itself in individual acts of its subject, and which is the master of the subjectivity; that it is *conscious* intention. This presupposition is false. Paul does not regard man as primarily a conscious subject. The tendencies of will and act which give man his characteristics are not his subjective strivings. Rather Paul regards humanity as transcending the sphere of its own consciousness. This is very clearly expressed in Paul's view that man wills and acts under the lordship of either the flesh or the spirit (e.g., Rom. 8:5ff; 8:12ff; Gal. 5:16ff). There is no third alternative. From the point of view of subjective anthropology these "forces" to which man is subject can be understood only as mythological entities or interpreted in terms of a naturalistic dualism. I hope that my interpretation of Romans 7 shows that these "forces" in reality designate the possibilities of historical existence.

First of all, it seems clear to me that the intention of which Paul is speaking is no more a movement of the will within the sphere of subjectivity than are—and this is certainly clear on the face of it—the "setting the mind" of Romans 8:5–7, 27 and the "desires" of Galatians 5:17.[5] This intention is the total tendency of human existence, and transcends subjectivity. I am confident that this will be evident when I show what it is toward which the intention is directed. Before I do this, however, I would like to deal with one more misunderstanding which often influences exegesis.

It is by no means the case that the doing of evil which we find in the conflict described in Romans 7:14 can be traced back to the flesh, while on the other hand the desire to do good arises from a force opposed to the flesh but powerless against it, a force such as "mind" or "inner man."[6] No, man himself is of the flesh precisely because he is characterized by the clash between his intentions and his actions. Both his intentions and his actions (v. 18) have their location in him, in his flesh. Intentions and actions are not distributed between different subjects—perhaps a better self as opposed to lower drives—but both are carried out by the same self. In the same way flesh and mind (inner man) are not two separate entities which together make up man. Man himself is this conflict.[7]

The objection may be raised that this passage shows that the "I" can divorce itself from the sin dwelling within, and that it can even disclaim responsibility for what is done (vv. 17, 20)! It is this apparently contradictory description—analagous to that in Galatians 2:19f—with its differentiation of the two elements while the "I" is the subject of both (vv. 14f, 20), which reveals the peculiar character of the situation. It is not a question of a struggle between two coexisting but separate subjects any more than of a tension between two forces. Man is divided and at war with himself because this situation should not and must not be; indeed, in view of his true nature, it cannot be. But this fact is valid because it is a question of the true nature of human existence, and man always falls short of achieving it.

It is clear that the "I" which takes its position over against sin—in other words, the inner man, the mind— is man insofar as he is aware of his true nature. Consciously or unconsciously his being is determined and driven by the fact that it is his true nature which is in question here. For Paul it is self-evident that knowing this and being controlled by God's claims are one and the same. Only when man is just in God's sight is he all that he should and can be.[8] Man is then a being who is concerned with his distinctive nature. He desires to express it in all his actions, but he can and (according to Paul) does fail in this. As a result he is victim of an inner division. In all his actions he is the one who is acting, because in his actions he seeks to achieve his distinctive nature. And yet insofar as he does not achieve it, *he* has *not* acted in his distinctive nature.

Let us look at the context briefly. Romans 1:18—3:20 shows that both Jews and heathen stand under the revelation of the righteousness of God and the wrath of God, that is, they are under sentence of death. Romans 3:21–31 states that God has opened a way of salvation through his righteousness, and chapter 4 gives the scriptural proof of this. Here, characteristically, God the object of faith is described as the giver of life (v. 17). What follows can be understood only if we keep in mind that for Paul as well as for Judaism righteousness is an eschatological blessing, and that Paul paradoxically declares that this eschatological blessing is now present. This is seen in chapter 5, which begins, "Therefore, since we are justified . . ." As a result, the question arises for Jewish thought and for

that of Paul as to where this salvation is to be found.
Where is life? What about death and sin? They seem to be
very much present, and their presence seems to make the
presence of righteousness illusory.

This discussion dominates chapters 5–8. Death and life
are the theme of chapter 5, and sin and sanctification the
theme of chapters 6:1—7:6. The discussion of the first
theme is the necessary preparation for the second, because
death and sin on the one hand and life and sanctification
(bearing fruit for God, 7:4) on the other belong together.
This is clearly seen in 7:1–6 where the inner relationship
of law and sin is made clear. No one can conclude on the
basis of the connection between death and sin, and life
and sanctification, as demonstrated in chapter 6, or from
the Christian's freedom from sin shown there, that after
the destruction of sin the law could still be preserved. Law
and sin (7:5) belong together and lead to death. Anyone
who is freed from sin (chap. 6) is also freed from the
law, and is placed in the state of "the new life of the
Spirit" (7:6). The argument is complete.

If 6:1–23 answered the question raised in 3:21 by
showing that sin is abolished together with the law, then
at the end of the argument in 7:1–6 the thesis is reversed;
the law is abolished along with sin. The point reached in
7:6 is taken up once more in 8:1, and the two great
themes of 5:1—7:6 are discussed again in a new form and
in reverse order. Chapter 8:1–11 discusses freedom from
sin, and 8:12–39 freedom from death. Here the relationship of the two themes to each other is made clear by the
fact that the second is stated at the conclusion of the
first (8:10f) and the first at the beginning of the second
(8:12f). They are related to each other as presupposition
and consequence. I do not intend to trace here the way

in which this repetition casts new light on these themes and their interrelationship, or to trace the details of their presentation. It is enough to say that the whole section substantiates the thesis that the blessing—life—is now present. The believer is already in possession of the future and, together with it, of the present blessing.

Then what is the meaning of the verses 7:7–25 that come between these two sections? They are, as has often been rightly said, an apology for the law.[9] They are to prevent the reader from saying, on the basis of 7:1–6 (especially v. 5), where law and sin are brought together, that "the law is sin" (v. 7). This apology is not motivated by either piety or deference to the shocked reader, but by the clear insight that the guilt of sin is forfeited once the law is no longer regarded as God's demand, since man's guilt results from his failure to fulfill that demand.

The "apology" in 7:7–13 shows that the commands of the law awaken the sin which has been lying dormant in man. It was precisely the will of God, good though it is, that led to man's death as a result of the sin which reigned within man. Verses 14–25 give a further clarification of this statement by showing how law and sin determine man's nature. This not only has the negative result of preventing false conclusions, but it also resumes the positive thought of verses 1–6. Verse 5 is shown to be correct and the inner relationship of law and sin is clarified, with the result that when Paul answers the question raised in 7:24 he also returns to the theme of 7:6.

For the details of interpretation we should keep clearly in mind the dominant idea expressed here, that we are basically dealing with an eschatological blessing and that the two eschatological possibilities are life and death. Thus the theme of 7:7, 14–25 is clearly formulated in

7:5: "While we were living in the flesh, our sinful passions, aroused by the law, were at work in our members
to bear fruit for death." The performance of the law is
always seen in terms of its result—death. What is developed more fully in verses 7ff is stated here: death is
the result of observing the law, because the law activates
sinful passions (covetousness, vv. 7f).

The emphasis in verses 7–13 is once more on the fact
that following the law results in death. The commandments[10] which are intended to lead to *life* lead instead
to *death* (v. 10). This is further developed in verses 11–13
(corresponding to v. 5). The law was the means by which
sin brought about death (v. 13). Verse 5 spoke of sinful
passions and verses 7f of covetousness. It is characteristic
here that Paul does not speak of transgressing the law.
He pays no attention to the problem of whether or to
what degree transgressions of the law occur while one is
following the law. Rather he stresses the fact that through
the commandments desires are aroused. They are aroused
regardless of whether a command is transgressed or fulfilled. Man is a sinner even when he keeps the commandments. Verse 6 shows clearly that Paul has in mind
following the law and not transgressions of the law. The
phrase "aroused by the law" which he uses here does not
have the primary meaning of making transgressions impossible, but as the ὥστε clause shows, the elimination of
serving "the old written code." This means release from
service of the law as such, from a service which results
in death, according to 2 Corinthians 3:6f. In the same
way freedom from following the law is characterized in
2 Corinthians 3:13 as "taking away" the law. It is clear
that in view of the line of thought in 3:21 and the
following passages, 7:1–6 can mean only deliverance

from legalism as such, that is, abolition of the law as a way of achieving salvation by works, not a setting aside of trespasses.

We must keep this in mind in discussing verses 14–25. Verse 13 told why the end of keeping the law is death, and verse 24 ends with the question, "Who will deliver me from this body of death?" In corresponding manner 8:1f describes the nature of existence in faith: "the law of the Spirit of life in Christ Jesus has set me free from the law of sin and death." In this new existence then the demands of the law can also come to fulfillment, but this is the case only if the direction of the path of law is reversed.

It should now be clear what Paul means by, "I do not understand my own actions" (v. 15). It means that man does not know that his serving "the old written code" leads to death, just as 2 Corinthians 3:14f says that the Jew does not know the significance of his keeping the law; his senses are dulled and a veil lies over the law. Here the significance of "I do not understand" becomes clear. In the usual interpretations it must always be explained in some artificial manner[11] such as, "I do not know why it is that my good intentions are always followed by transgressions," or "I am acting in an incomprehensible manner" (Lietzmann). As a result, the "working" here, just as in verse 13 where it was used in connection with sin, is comparable to the "intention" (see above). That is, it does not refer to the empirical act of transgression but to the result of the act, which is the same for every act of the one who is under law: death.

Now the dichotomy in verses 15–20 is clear. The object of man's intention is life, but the result of what he does is death. Life is what is good and right, and death is the evil

(vv. 19, 21). Because of the intentionally sententious and antithetical formulation these entities appear as objects of the verb "do" even though life and death are not "done" or "made." It can be seen that the verbs translated "do" must be interpreted in terms of "working" (κατεργάζεσθαι) when we note that this verb occurs repeatedly (vv. 17, 18, 20), and that it means, as it usually does in Paul's writings but not always elsewhere, to achieve, to produce (cf. v. 13). Paul chose the verbs ποιεῖν and πράσσειν because he wished to express in as pointed a manner as possible the inner contradiction between the desire and the deed, between the intention and the act. All action is *a priori* directed against its own proper intention. *This* is the conflict! It is the same problem which was formulated in verse 10: "the very commandment which promised life proved to be death to me." *This* is the riddle, the solution of which we see when faith opens our eyes to the nature of sin: the real intent of the law is corrupted into its opposite, into actual idolatry. It is now clear what is meant by συνφάναι and συνήδεσθαι τῷ νόμῳ (vv. 16, 22)—not acceptance of the concrete demands of the law in a specific situation, but the affirmation of its basic intention, which is to lead to life.[12]

Paul's whole concept becomes clear when we ask, as we are now able to do, how we are to understand sin as something which, already present in man, can be awakened by the "law." Law confronts man as God's claim, "Thou shalt (not)!" In other words, law would keep man from having his own say. Consequently, sin is man's desire to have his own say, to lay claim to himself, to be like God.[13] Because this sin produces death it becomes clear first that man, wishing to be himself, loses himself; sin replaces the "I" as the subject (v. 9), and second that it is part of man's nature to be himself, because when he is no longer himself he dies (v. 9f). That is to say, he cannot be himself if he seeks to do so in his own strength, if he seeks to assert himself, but only if he surrenders himself, if he yields to God's claim, if he is dependent on God. That would bring him life, and he would thus achieve his true nature.[14] It is precisely man's desire to achieve this true nature which causes him to lose it. This is the deception which sin practices on us (v. 11). But because the desire for realizing one's true nature is contained in the desire to assert oneself, although disguised and distorted, it is possible to speak of the dichotomy in such a way as to contrast the true self with the actual self.

For this reason verses 7–13 do not portray "the psychological process by which individual sins occur in man" (Lietzmann), but the process which forms the basis for the entire existence under law, and which lies beyond subjectivity and psychic processes. The possibility of sin consists in the fact that man is a self who is concerned about his true nature, and that he finds his true nature (as a creature) only when he yields to God's claims. The possibility of a misunderstanding lies in the fact that God's claim is *a priori* directed toward man's true nature. On his own terms man wants to be the one called to fulfill his true nature.

Finally, because Romans 7:7–25 deals with suprapersonal events it is possible to understand Romans 7 in its relationship to 5:12–21. But I cannot deal with this here, nor can I take the opportunity to draw further conclusions, either positive insights or new questions, from the material developed in this essay.

NOTES

1. Werner Georg Kümmel, *Römer 7 und die Bekehrung des Paulus* (1929).

2. Quoted by Lietzmann in his Romans commentary. Jülicher thinks it is a question of practicing works against which our conscience protests. In the same way Zahn speaks of the conflict of desire and deed. See also Weinel, *Biblische Theologie des N.T.*, 4th ed., p. 223. Gerhardt Kuhlmann has rightly protested against this view in *Theologia naturalis bei Philon und bei Paulus* (1930), p. 104.

3. Adolf Schlatter, *Der Glaube im N.T.*, 4th ed., 1927, p. 331.

4. Cf. Wilhelm Mundle, "Das religiöse Problem des 4. Esrabuches," *ZAW*, N.F. 6 (1929), pp. 222-249.

5. It is clear in Romans 8:27 that the mind of the spirit which fills the one praying and determines his character is concealed from man and understood only by God.

6. Verse 25*b* could be misinterpreted in this way. But if this statement is not an explanatory gloss, as I believe it to be, it must be interpreted in the light of the preceding material. Cf. Kümmel, *op. cit.*, pp. 67f.

7. As Kümmel rightly saw, *op. cit.*, pp. 134ff.

8. I do not see why Kümmel, *op. cit.*, p. 137, denies that "mind" expresses the idea that man is subject to God's claims, because he admits that according to Paul the mind should recognize God's commands. What does this mean except that "mind" expresses the possibility of man's being subject to God? When God says, "Thou shalt!" it is something quite different from a woodcutter's saying a tree shall be chopped down. This "shall" does not determine the tree's mode of being, but God's "Thou shalt" determines man's. In *Theologia naturalis bei Philon und bei Paulus*, Kuhlmann strips Paul's concept of sin of its historical character. He cannot recognize that man as "inner man" hears God's claims. But I do not understand why Kuhlmann thinks that if this is so, "inner man" implies the justification of the "natural man" (p. 106, 1). On the contrary, this is the basis of the possibility of condemnation, of death. If the tree is cut down it does not "die."

9. Cf. Kümmel, *op. cit.*, p. 9.

10. On the concept "commandment," see Kümmel, *op. cit.*, pp. 55f.

11. I wish to cite here a statement from a paper written for

a seminar by Karl Erdmann. "If verse 15*b* is read as containing a dualistic contrast between good intentions and evil deeds, it is impossible to bring it into an intelligible relation to verse 15*a*. Such a psychic tension would bring with it the intense consciousness of the chasm which divides the ideal intent from the deed corrupted by the material world. Romans 7:24, taken as a cry of deliverance expressive of this tension, does not lend itself to any illusion about the real state of affairs. It would be meaningless to take 15*b* as the basis for 15*a*: 'I do not understand my own actions.' Thus Lietzmann regards it as 'a merely rhetorical expression.' The interrelationship of the parts of the statement becomes clear only when it is seen as the Christian's condemnation of his former unbelief. His new insight into the sinfulness of the striving for righteousness shows that inasmuch as the will wants to achieve righteousness it produces precisely what it did not intend: sin, separation from God. The inner breach of which verse 15 is speaking does not exist between man's intentions and his acts, but within his understanding of himself in relation to God."

12. This discussion shows why I must reject as false Kuhlmann's interpretation of Paul. Because he regards sin in Paul's writings only as something negative, a godlessness, and not as the positive relationship which man as sinner bears to God, the law signifies for him not God's continuing, distinct claim, but only a possibility confronting sinful man; in other words, the possibility of conscience to be subject to the idea of the "good." Because Kuhlmann sees correctly that the conflict depicted in Romans 7:14ff is not to be understood in terms of good intentions and evil deeds, he is at a loss how to explain what the evil is that appears in the deed. It is certainly not transgression of the law. How can man "experience" that "what he has performed to the best of his intentions and in good conscience is still evil"? He would have to assume that evil was "the manner in which influence was brought to bear on the 'other' man." "If a man performs the good as he knows it, he inevitably finds in the resistance of his 'neighbor' that in relation to the other person it is nothing but evil." Even though "he does the good with all the seriousness of his being" he cannot "keep from doing evil to his neighbor" (p. 104, 1). It is not clear how such a person would conceive of the concept "neighbor" and how it is possible for him, in the light of his idea of good, to regard as evil his actions which are directed against his neighbor's resistance. Besides this, the text does not at all say that man "finds" as evil that which he does. Rather the words "I do not understand" say the opposite of this. But all in all this

is a completely unpauline idea which has been imposed on Romans 7.

13. If Paul is really thinking of Adam in verses 7–13, then he is expressing specifically the desire to be like God; but see Kümmel, *op. cit.,* p. 54.

14. That the concept of "true nature" is not foreign to the passage but is a relevant expression of what Paul means is shown, for example, when Lietzmann casually says in connection with verse 9 that the ζῆν of which Paul is speaking is life "in the true sense of the word." What does it mean when exegetes speak repeatedly of life in the "pregnant" sense of the word? What else but the true nature of the self?

III

Adam and Christ
in Romans 5

In 1952 Karl Barth published in *Theologische Studien* an interpretation of the fifth chapter of Romans entitled "Christ and Adam in Romans 5." Since he once stated that theological disputes must be decided in the light of exegesis it seems to me proper to investigate critically his exegesis of Romans 5. I do not intend to do this by discussing his work step by step, but rather by placing my interpretation of Romans 5 and his side by side in order to go into Barth's exegesis critically after interpreting each of the two major sections, Romans 5:1–11 and 5:12–21. I am prefacing the interpretation of each section by a translation, which, since it contains a certain amount of interpretation, can be an aid in the detailed exegesis.[1]

The theme, or rather the problem, dealt with in Romans 5 grows out of the preceding chapters. It is the assurance of the future (eschatological) life of the one who has been justified. A brief summary may make this clear.

1:18—3:20. Heathen and Jew both are confronted by the revelation of the righteousness of God and both are under the wrath of God.

3:21–31. The salvation event accomplished by Christ has made righteousness available through faith.

4:1–15. Here is the scriptural proof of this thesis. Since righteousness is an eschatological blessing which includes life, and since Paul asserts that it is a present reality, he must answer the questions: "Is life now present? Is it not rather death and sin that are present?" Romans 5:1–21 is the answer to the question whether life is a present reality.

I

Romans 5:1–11 contains the first proof of the presence of life. It is an argument from the greater to the lesser. If righteousness is present reality, then, all the more, life is present too. The passage shows that life is present in hope.[2]

1. Since we have now been justified by faith, we have peace with God through our Lord Jesus Christ,

2. through whom we have received access (by faith?) to this grace, in which we have won our stand, and we exult in the hope of the glory of God.

3. And that is not all! And we exult in hardships (we know that hardship produces patience,

4. and patience character, and character hope,

5. and hope does not let us down), for the love of God has been poured out in our hearts by the Holy Spirit, whom we have received as a gift.

6. For when we were still weak, when we were still without God, Christ died for us.

7. For one will hardly die for a righteous man, but one may dare to die for a good man.

8. But God established the proof of his love for us by Christ's dying for us while we were still sinners.

9. Now that we have been made righteous by his blood we will certainly be saved by him from the judgment of wrath.

10. For if when we were enemies we were reconciled with

God through the death of his son, then as those who have been reconciled we will much more be saved through his life. 11. That is not all! We exult in God through our Lord Jesus Christ, through whom we have now been reconciled.

VERSE 1. The results of justification on the basis of faith are described first of all as peace with God. This is of course not "peace of mind," because all psychological characteristics of salvation are foreign here. It is an objectively new situation, a new relationship between God and men (believing men) which God has effected through Christ. The previous relationship was one of enmity ("we were enemies," v. 10). This is one of being reconciled. That is what is meant by peace—the reconciliation which God accomplished. It is not something men have brought about; they can make it their own only in faith (cf. 2 Cor. 5:20, "we beseech you . . .").

Strictly speaking, the reconciliation is the result of righteousness, according to verse 1. But in actuality it is reconciliation or peace which results in righteousness. Thus the "justified" of verse 1 is taken up again in verses 10f by "we were reconciled . . ." In 3:24 righteousness is accomplished by Christ; in 5:11 he is the one "through whom we have now been reconciled." According to 1:16f the gospel reveals the "righteousness of God," and according to 2 Corinthians 5:19 it is the "message of reconciliation."

VERSE 2. The words "through whom we have received access . . ." really are only repeating what was said by "justified." The grace to which Christ has given us access and in which we stand by faith is precisely that state which Christ has brought about. Just as man should accept reconciliation (2 Cor. 5:20), so he should also accept grace (2 Cor. 6:1). To forsake the way of faith would mean negating the grace of God (Gal. 2:21), falling from grace (Gal. 5:4).

"And we exult in the hope of the glory of God." This is really the answer to the question that casts its shadow on the whole chapter; the present is a time of hope! It is hope for the future eschatological salvation, which is often described as "glory" (cf. 2 Cor. 4:17) and is here called the "glory of God" (subjective or qualitative genitive). The description of the "others" as those "who have no hope" is an indication that this hope is a positive one (1 Thess. 4:13). Paul does not mean a plain hope such as is common to all, but a hope that is certain to be fulfilled and which "does not let us down" (v. 5).

"Glory" then is not present, but future, anticipated by faith. Verse 3 tells us what effect this hope has on the present.

VERSE 3. "And we exult in hardships" (note the "and"). Thus a paradox characterizes the Christian's present state. In Judaism too there is a boasting in suffering because suffering brings merit. There it is a result of the uncertainty and anxiety of existence. Here for Paul it is a result of certainty. The one who believes does not need merit, because he has already been justified, or as verse 8 explains it, "by Christ's dying . . ."

This reason is supplemented by a statement in apposition, which is best read as parenthetical: "we know that hardship produces patience"! How do we know this? The sentence should be taken as a general truth, or even as a proverb which like many proverbs can be understood in two ways. Here then hardship can produce patience, or, more in keeping with the context, the meaning of hardship is the production of patience.

VERSE 4. "And patience [produces] character, and character hope." This is a chain or progression, the climax of which is hope. It would seem here that hope is only the result of a movement which leads from patience, through character, to hope, but in verse 2 hope is something that is given along with justifying faith. This only underlines the fact that faith is not static, and hope no assured possession. Faith is a direction of life which must always be preserved in patience and must be continuously renewed so that hope is always attained afresh.

In reference to the main problem we note the following points: (1) The believer lives constantly (only) in hope, that is to say, not on the basis of what he possesses, but by reason of what he will receive—he lives in relation to the future. Consequently he always has hope and the present is always only temporary. (2) But it is this that is the fruit of faith—the ability to regard what is present as something passing. It is freedom from present reality, immunity from the tribulations which plunge the unbeliever into anxiety. It is freedom from the anxiety that constantly threatens life; it is being open to the future. The paradoxical character of being a Christian which is expressed in "we exult" is therefore the same as that which Paul describes in 2 Corinthians 4:7–11 (cf. 2 Cor. 6:9f; 12:9f).

Luther explained this cogently in his lectures on Romans in 1516–1517: "Quia qui habet fidem, omnia illa quidem habet, sed abscondite. Per tribulationem autem exercentur ad eminentiam" (Ficker edition, Gloss 46, pp. 17f). And also "Qualia et qualem invenit tribulatio, talia et talem magis facit" (Schol. 133, 14f). "Ad hanc igitur probationem non pervenitur nisi per patientiam. Et fit ista examinatio, ut appareat unicuique suus affectus, i.e. ut quisque cognoscat se ipsum, utrum sc. vere Deum propter Deum diligat, quod Deus sine examinatione cognoscit" (Schol. 136, 16ff. See also 137 for the difference between *spes* and *presumptio*).

VERSE 5. The certainty of hope finds its expression in the statement "and hope does not let us down." This is relevant whether it is based on the following statement ("for the love of God . . .") or on (bridging the parenthesis of 3b–5a) the "we exult" of verse 3a.

When Paul says of the love of God (subjective genitive) that it "has been poured . . ." and names the Spirit as the mediator, it is obvious that two thoughts have been combined. It would have been simpler to say, "because the Holy Spirit has been poured out in our hearts." The Spirit is the "first fruits" (8:23), the "guarantee" (2 Cor. 1:22) of the eschatological future. The thought would then be clearly expressed as: "Hope cannot deceive, because we already have the down payment on the future and are therefore already to some degree in the eschatological existence." (Here it is inconsequential whether Paul is thinking of our receiving the Spirit in baptism, or of his activity in the congregation, of ecstatic experiences, or of the working of the Spirit in our daily Christian life.) In any case this is what Paul meant to say, as otherwise his mentioning the Spirit in this context would not have any meaning. According to the context, verse 5 can only mean that we are assured of God's love, which as verses 6–8 explain makes us righteous through Christ. Since this includes the certainty of the future fulfillment of salvation (vv. 9f) it is identical with our knowledge that we have received the Spirit. In verse 5 then, Paul is saying these two things at the same time: that we have the Spirit, and that we know God's love. Both are the basis of the hope, and of the "we exult." Together they form a unity, because the Spirit brings the assurance of God's love. Verses 6–8 show that we can speak of the love of God in this connection.

VERSE 6. God's love was made manifest in that Christ died for us. The death of Christ on our behalf is characterized by the clause "when we were still weak." Then Paul adds by way of clarification, "when we were still without God, Christ died for us." Both ideas are expressed again by the words "while we were still sinners" in verse 8 and "when we were enemies" in verse 10. Verse 7 expresses how astonishing and magnificent this is.

VERSE 7. Hardly anyone would die for a "righteous man," although perhaps he would for a "good man." It is difficult to distinguish between these two, just as it is hard to distinguish between "weak" and "without God" in verse 6, and between "sinners" in verse 8 and "enemies" in verse 10. The second statement is clearly designed only as a narrowing of the scope of the first. We are not supposed to reflect whether there may be exceptions. As a rule, this is the case, and these statements are designed to express the amazing nature of Christ's death for us sinners.

VERSE 8. This verse says that Christ's death for sinners is the proof of God's love, substantiating what was said in verse 5, and verse 9 goes on to show its consequences for Paul's line of thought. We can be certain of the completion of our salvation; hope has a firm basis.

VERSE 9. Much more then is it true that "we will be saved . . ." Here we are once again made aware of the basis of God's love as stated in verses 6f, but in such a way that the emphasis lies not on its amazing nature, but on its result, or on the meaning of Christ's death: "we have been made righteous by his blood." It is thus our justification that was achieved by Christ's death. Instead of saying "through his death," as we might expect from verses 6–8 and as he does say in verse 10, Paul uses a traditional formula, "by his blood." We may compare this with 3:25 where Paul follows a similar formula. Except for these two passages and the traditional formulation of the eucharist, Paul does not speak of the blood, but of the death, or of the cross of Christ.

His certainty about the future is now expressed by the words "we will certainly be saved by him from the judgment of wrath." This means salvation from the wrathful judgment which precedes the eschatological culmination. (Wrath here is to be taken in as objective a sense as "peace" is in verse 1.)

VERSE 10. The "for" does not give the basis for verse 9; rather, 9 and 10 are parallel, and the "for" gives an additional basis for verse 5. "We were reconciled with God" corresponds to "we have been made righteous" in verse 9, just as "through the death of his son" corresponds to "by his blood." Paul is stressing the astonishing and significant element here by the words "if when we were enemies." In this verse "enemies" replaces the "weak" and "without God" of verse 6 and the "sinners" of verse 8. In 8:7 "enemies" has the active meaning of "showing enmity toward," but here, as in 11:28, it apparently has the passive sense of "odious to." But it is difficult to separate the two meanings.

The conclusion "much more" is the same as in verse 9. The words "we will be saved" are defined more closely not by saying what we are delivered from, as in verse 9, but by stating the means: "through his life." The ἐν is to be read as instrumental, and the words "through his life" correspond to "through [his] death." By formulating it this way Paul shows that for him it is obvious that Christ's death and his resurrection belong together. His death gained its decisive significance by the resurrection. Thus instead of "through his life" Paul could have said "through his resurrection." Compare 4:25 and especially 2 Corinthians 4:14.

VERSE 11. The development of thought is now complete, but Paul never tires of expressing the assurances of Christian hope. He here reintroduces (casually, by using the participial form of "exult"; cf. 3:24) the motif of exulting which he used in verses 2f, and the "and that is not all" of verse 3. The exulting is not in the specific terms of verse 3, "in hardships," nor even the more general expression of verse 2, "in the hope of the glory of God," but the most general expression possible, one which includes everything else, "in God." All other exulting is indeed based on God. Paul expresses this by stating that the exulting is mediated "through our Lord Jesus Christ." The "through" here does not refer, as in verses 1f, to the origin, but to the one who mediates, and this is in keeping with liturgical usage. The congregation, however, can praise God with exulting "through Christ" because this praise is based on Christ. This is further expressed in the clause "through whom we have now been reconciled." This is the same as to say that through him we have obtained "peace" and "access to this grace." Thus the thought of verses 1–11 is rounded out. And by so doing Paul brings to light in the "now" the new situation, which contrasts with "when we were still weak . . ." (Compare this with the "now" in 2 Cor. 5:16.)

The paradoxical eschatological nature of the future of the believer is made clear in 5:1–11, and as a result the question of whether "life" is present is answered provisionally. But is not the presence of "life" only relative, that is to say, is it not merely anticipated in "hope"? It is obvious that Paul feels required to express more clearly the fact that "life" is present, and he does this in 5:12–21.

Barth's interpretation of 5:1–11 presents the thought of the passage correctly inasmuch as he finds here the idea that the basis of Christian hope is in the death and resurrection of Jesus. It should be noted that Barth places more emphasis on the resurrection, which is only alluded to in verse 10, than on the death, which is stressed in the text (vv. 6–9, and especially in v. 10). Barth is also right in saying that Paul speaks here of an objective saving event. God's love "did not then wait for us, but came to us in anticipation" (p. 2).[3] "If they [men] believe, then they are only *following* the decision already made for them in him [Christ]" (p. 3).

But Barth does not interpret the passage in terms of its context in the epistle, and therefore not in the light of the main question of the presence of salvation, of life. What interests him is the relationship of man to Christ, and he believes that he must conclude from the text that Christ as an individual human being includes all other human beings within himself. In faith "they perceive and realize that precisely this history of his is in reality their own; that *their* essential history can be only something like a retracing and a copy of his" (p. 4). This means "that he is in them, and they are in him, even before they are confronted by the question of the status of their love for God" (p. 4). It would be interesting to know how Barth understands this "being in" since it is formulated in the same manner as the gnostic doctrine of primordial man.

Barth interprets the passage this way because he is

already looking at 5:12–21 where such a christology is indeed present, but in 5:1–11 the dominant thought is that of substitution or sacrifice (for those "without God" v. 6 and "for us" v. 8, "by his blood" v. 9). The christology of 5:12–21, which Barth reads into 5:1–11, is in fact gnostic, but in 5:1–11 christological doctrine is formulated in terms of the cultic and juristic concepts of Jewish tradition.

But quite apart from the fact that Barth obviously overlooks this distinction, he makes a major theme out of what is really only a minor motif. The real theme of 5:1–11 is the paradoxical existence of believers in hope.

II

Romans 5:12–21 gives the second proof. Adam and Christ; the former is the bringer of death, the latter the bringer of life.

12. Therefore (it is true that) as sin entered the world through *one* man and through sin, death, and in this way death gained sway over all men, because all sinned
13. —for until the law sin was in the world; sin is not charged at all against anyone when there is no law.
14. But (in spite of this) death reigned from Adam until Moses even over those who had not sinned in a way comparable to the transgression of Adam, who is a prefiguring of the coming (Adam).
15. But the case is not the same with the gift of grace as it was with the trespass. For if as a result of the trespass of one, many died, so the grace of God and the gracious gift of the one man Jesus Christ have come all the more abundantly to the many.
16. And it is not the same with the gift as (the case was) with the one who sinned. For (judgment) came as a result of one person (or: as the result of one trespass?) and led to

condemnation. The gracious gift however (follows) many transgressions and (leads) to vindication.

17. For if, through the trespass of one, death came to reign through that one, then all the more those who receive the abundant grace and the gift of justification will come to reign in life through the one man, Jesus Christ.

18. Now then, since as a result of one trespass all men came under condemnation, so it (comes), as a result of one act of righteousness, that all men have justification, which is (means? brings?) life.

19. For as through the disobedience of one man many became sinners, so also through the obedience of one man many will become justified.

20. But the law came in between the two events so that the trespass would be multiplied. But wherever sin multiplied, there grace was even more abundant,

21. in order that, just as sin reigned through death, so grace might also reign through righteousness to eternal life, through Jesus Christ our Lord.

VERSE 12. The thought of the sentence is not carried through. The "as" has nothing corresponding to it in a subsequent clause and is only taken up as an afterthought by the "as" in verse 18. Then the sentence is interrupted by a parenthetical statement in verses 13f. But after that, instead of the expected analogy of Adam and Christ expressed by "as . . . so" we have first a description of the contrast in the analogy in the form "but not as . . . as" (v. 15).

Verse 12 says that through "one man," Adam, sin was brought into the world (that is, into human history) and as a result, death became the fate of all men. The real point of the sentence is not to show the origin of sin but the origin of death as a foil for the actual theme of the section: the origin of (new) life. For, in the context, the theme of verses 12–21 demonstrates that life is a present reality, or that life is a certainty for all who are Christian. Just as through Adam death was brought on adamic mankind, so through Christ life has been brought to mankind. But since for Paul death is the punishment or the consequence of sin, he must also speak of Adam's sin.

It is characteristic that Paul is not concerned with showing the origin of Adam's sin. For him it consists of Adam's trespass (vv. 15–17) or his disobedience (v. 19). The Genesis story is in the background. Neither sin nor the death of mankind is there traced back to Adam's sin, as Genesis 3 plays no role at all in the Old Testament. It was only in later Judaism that Adam's fall was given the significance of having brought sin and death into the world (4 Esdras, Syriac Baruch, Rabbinical sources cited in Strack-Billerbeck, Vol. III, pp. 227f). Paul assumes this as something well known. But by leaving aside the Jewish ideas about Satan as the cause of sin and death and of evil drives, Paul keeps to the simple thought: sin came into the world through sinning. Paul does not reflect here on the idea that sin was already latent in Adam and was awakened and made real by God's commandment (7:7–11). Much less does he reflect on the view that Adam was ψυχικός and χοϊκός (1 Cor. 15:44–49) and was totally unable to comprehend God's commandment. (Compare Rom. 7:14, "the law is spiritual.") As "dust" (χοϊκός) Adam was *a priori* subject to death and did not need to sin at all to become so.

The "therefore" which connects verse 12 to verses 1–11 can be understood as follows: Because we have received our reconciliation through Christ it is true that Christ, the bringer of life, is the contrast to Adam, the bringer of death. But verses 12–21 are not intended as a mere conclusion drawn from verses 1–11, but a further development of the idea of life as something present, a second proof of this. The "therefore" is then probably nothing more than a transitional phrase.

Since in the context the important thing is only that Adam brought death into the world, the explanatory clause "because all sinned" is really superfluous. In itself the $\grave{\epsilon}\varphi'$ $\tilde{\dot{\omega}}$ could be read as masculine just as well as neuter—"because of him" or "as a result of his action." But in such a case Adam would have to be specifically mentioned. Death is said to have come into the world as the result of Adam's sin! Yes, the statement creates confusion; for while in verse 12 the responsibility for sin and death falls on Adam, it is now ascribed to sinful man. It is conceivable that Paul, for whom death is the result of sin, is speaking also of the sin of those on whom Adam brought death.

VERSES 13–14. The difficulty is increased by these two verses. They set out to support the statement "because all sinned" by saying that after Adam sin and then death also reigned over mankind. On the other hand, Paul wants to emphasize the distinction between the sins of mankind after Adam and Adam's sin when he says, "for until the law sin was in the world;"—that is, immediately after Adam there was sin in the world—"sin is not charged at all against anyone when there is no law." But how can Paul say that "sin is not charged against anyone" when it clearly has death as its consequence? There is no answer to this. Paul clearly intends to say that sin from Adam to Moses was of a different type from that of Adam. Verse 14 expresses this when it describes sinners before Moses' day as not having sinned in the way Adam did. But can there be a sin that is not "trespass" (or "disobedience," v. 19)?

Here then the confusion increases. (1) The basic thought that the nature of adamic humanity was determined by Adam, who brought sin and death into the world, is undermined by the clause "because all sinned." (2) The sin of Adam is distinguished from the sin of pre-Mosaic humanity in an impossible manner, because the law is what makes sin really sinful.

All this confusion is the result of the fact that the parallel of Adam and Christ, that is, the idea of two humanities, or two epochs of humanity, each one determined by the one who begins it, is a gnostic idea conceived in terms of cosmology and not in terms of salvation history. It is seen in its pure form in 1 Corinthians 15:21f:

> For as by a man came death,
>> by a man has come also the resurrection of the dead.
> For as in Adam all die,
>> so also in Christ shall all be made alive.

In the same manner, 1 Corinthians 15:47f:

> The first man was from the earth, a man of dust;
>> the second man is from heaven.
> As was the man of dust, so are those who are of the dust;
>> and as is the man of heaven, so are those who are of heaven.

Here it is not a question of sin as the occasion for death or a question of law. Death is seen here in gnostic terms as a fate which is common to all mankind descended from primordial man.

It is clear that Paul is not satisfied with his description

of life in 5:1–11 as something already possessed by anticipation through hope. Rather he wants to present it as something already achieved through Christ. In Christ it is, although absent, already a present reality, even though it will be actualized for the individual only in the future (vv. 17, 19). He takes up the gnostic myth of primordial man in order to be able to express the present reality of life. He modifies it, first through the words "because all sinned," verse 12, and second by using salvation history to modify cosmological statements when he reflects on the significance of the law for adamic man.

As a result of the mixing of secondary ideas with it, the primary idea itself is expressed rather awkwardly in a relative clause that is tacked on: "who is a prefiguring of the coming (Adam)." This clause could stand as the heading of the entire passage. It would properly be followed by the positive sequel to the "as" in verse 12, but instead Paul lays stress first of all on the dissimilarity within the similarity. To be sure, this does not make the main idea any clearer, but it does give expression to the splendor of the figure of Christ and his gifts, and to his superiority over Adam.

VERSE 15. "But the case is not the same with the gift of grace as it was with the trespass." In this dogmatic formulation of the contrast the expressions are not in clear opposition to each other. For either "obedience" should be given as the contrast to "trespass," or "judgment" or "condemnation" as the contrast to "gift of grace." But it is clear that when Paul speaks of trespass he has its consequences in mind, and that when he speaks of the gift of grace he is conscious of its presuppositions.

We have here a twofold statement of the contrast. "For if as a result of the trespass . . . so all the more . . ."

Once again we do not have an exact formulation of the antithesis. We would naturally expect the contrast of Adam and Christ to be stated in a manner similar to that of verse 18. However in correspondence to "the trespass of one" we do not have "the obedience of one," but over against the "one" (Adam) stands God whose "gracious gift" (χάρις) contrasts to Adam's trespass. Still, this expresses the fact that what Christ accomplished by his obedience has its basis in God himself, because the result of obedience is mentioned at once and is parallel to God's grace: "and the gracious gift . . ." It is evident from the context with its antithesis of Adam and Christ that this gracious gift is life. In addition, the contrast of "many died" with "have come abundantly to the many" is also an inexact formulation. Yet this too is not a distortion of the thought since the gift which the many received is life itself. In this we should not lose sight of the fact that here, following Semitic usage, "the many" is the same as "all" in verses 12 and 18. Compare also the variation in verses 18–19.

While the result clauses in verses 17, 19 (21) are in the future tense, here the verb is a comprehensive aorist, "have come abundantly." Thus the relationship of Adam to Christ is formulated without reference to the (still unfulfilled) realization, just as it is in the sentence in verse 18, where there is no expression of tense.

The consequence of the clause beginning "for if" is not a simple correspondence (if one thing is true, then so is the other), but "all the more." We do not have a simple antithetical parallel between Adam and Christ. But why does Paul say "all the more"? Perhaps this is based on the Jewish concept that good is so much more powerful than evil (4 Esdras 4:30–32; Sifre 5:17. See also Strack-

Billerbeck, Vol. III, pp. 230, 120*a*). But possibly the idea here is that the effect of Christ's obedience is all the more powerful because it is a countereffect which must overcome the resistance of the existing situation, while the effect of Adam's fall did not encounter any obstacle.

VERSE 16. The "for" clause of verse 16 is parallel to the "for" clause of verse 15. Here however we do not simply have the gift or the gracious gift contrasted to Adam's sin. Rather, the sequel, which explains the first clause, "and it is not . . . ," is based on the clause "as a result of one . . . many transgressions." In Adam's line then one trespass stands at the beginning, and at the beginning of Christ's line, many. The antithesis of Adam (trespass) and Christ (gracious gift) is thereby somewhat distorted, apparently for the purpose of elucidating the "all the more" of verse 15, which is picked up again in verse 17. We may ask whether ἐκ (ἐξ) has a different meaning when used with "one" from that which it has with "many trespasses"; that is, a temporal meaning in the former case "as a result of one," while in the latter it would mean "although many trespasses were at hand."

A further distortion occurs when the explanatory clause speaks of, not Adam's trespass, but the condemnation of this trespass. We find judgment (κρίμα), and as a result, instead of the death of the many, condemnation (κατάκριμα). Here we should distinguish between judgment and condemnation, but κρίμα often includes the idea of condemnation, and in this passage the idea of condemnation is dominant. Paul probably varied his choice of words because he wished to characterize the condemnation of the many as something more comprehensive than the condemnation of Adam. Moreover, his probable reason for introducing the terms "judgment" and "condemnation" is that for him the concepts "life" and "righteousness" are intimately related. He thus brings in the idea of "righteousness"—in the form δικαίωμα, in contrast to κατάκριμα. This corresponds to the whole train of thought from 1:17 on, and especially to 3:21.

However, since Paul has spoken of judgment instead of Adam's trespass he cannot refer in the antithesis to Christ's obedience, but only to the gracious gift made possible by this obedience. Moreover, he has to give "vindication" as the antithesis of "condemnation" even though the gracious gift itself is vindication.

VERSE 17. This "for if" clause parallels the similar clause in verse 15 and that beginning with "for" in verse 16. The purport is again to clarify the antithesis of Adam and Christ in the same sense as "much more" in verse 15. The content of the clause "for if . . . death came to reign" corresponds to the "for if" clause of verse 15, and the "for (judgment) came as a result of one person and led to condemnation" of verse 16. Unlike verse 16, however, the contrast between the "one" and the "many" is no longer expressed, for the "one" appears only in the first clause. The stress falls much more on the contrast between death and life and the words "all the more" emphasize again the dominance of life over death.

It is quite remarkable that the obedience of Christ is not contrasted here to Adam's trespass, but instead persons are mentioned to whom this obedience brought life, "those who receive the abundant grace." The word "abundant" continues the idea "abundantly" of verse 15, and the expression "grace and the gift of justification" picks up again the idea of "grace and gracious gift" in verse 15. Verse 16 had already prepared the way for justification to be mentioned here instead of life, but Paul shows that the two belong together by the expression "to reign in life," where "reign" is in contrast to "death reigned" (v. 14).

The future tense of the verb "reign" brings out the idea that the realization of the life which Christ has already gained for us is still in the future. At the same time the paradoxical nature of the Christian situation is expressed in the words "those who receive." This receiving, which occurs in faith, is a present act.

At the same time the passage contains the hint that (in contrast to the gnostic myth) mankind after Christ is not bound to him by a natural bond, in the manner of 1 Corinthians 15:22 (see above), which corresponds to the myth. There the clause "in Christ shall all be made alive" is valid according to 15:23 only for those who belong to Christ. But there is then a basic difference between Adam and Christ which Paul has not pointed out. For adamic man there was no choice between life and death, but all were subject to death. The logical consequence would have to be that after Christ all men receive life. Naturally this is not what Paul means. Rather, all men must now decide whether they want to belong to those who receive it, presupposing that the word of proclamation has reached them. While Adam brought death on all mankind after him without any possibility of their escaping, Christ has brought a possibility that is open to all.

One thing is now clear. The destiny of adamic man was determined by Adam's trespass, but the destiny of mankind after Christ is not determined in the same way by Christ's obedience; it depends on the decision of faith to receive it. But now the destiny of those who do receive is determined. They are no longer in the position of the Jews who must achieve life by their own efforts, by works. They are assured of life. It is already there for them. Just as Adam's fall, which was determinative for adamic man, occurred before adamic man existed, so Christ's obedience and the gracious gift (v. 15), vindication and the gift of righteousness (v. 16), are there before these men exist, are theirs prior to all their strivings. Condemnation results because all individuals sinned (v. 12), but righteousness does not result because individual men were obedient as Christ was. Rather, it is only to be received as something which Christ has accomplished. Prevenient grace!

Finally, after the presentation of the dissimilarity of the parallel of Adam and Christ and the demonstration of the significance of Christ, Paul takes up again in verse 18 in the words "Now then, since as . . ." the "as" of verse 12.

VERSE 18. The antithetical parallelism of Christ and Adam is now carried through exactly with "as . . . so." Here it is a contrast not of the persons but of their actions: trespass and act of righteousness—and of the consequences: condemnation and acquittal and life. (Is the genitive epexegetical or objective?) The parallelism is expressed by the repetition of "one . . . all men." It goes without saying that condemnation consists of death. In verse 16 condemnation was balanced by justification, and here Paul says "justification" and "life" in order to stress again the concept δικαιοσύνη. Since he has just used the term δικαίωμα in the sense of "act of righteousness" he chooses here the form δικαίωσις.

VERSE 19. This verse is parallel to verse 18 and gives an additional basis for Paul's conclusions by using the concepts "disobedience" and "obedience" instead of "trespass" and "act of righteousness." The former terms are probably more concrete. The results of these contrasting actions are described by "became sinners" on the one hand, and "will become justified" on the other. If the use of the future tense is not due simply to the influence of the turning point in time, it may express the characteristic of "life" as something in the future, as in verse 17.

The words "will become justified" naturally do not mean "they will be regarded in the same way as those who are righteous," but "they will be made righteous." In the same way adamic men were not regarded as sinful, but as a result of Adam's disobedience they actually became sinners. δικαιοσύνη does not denote an ethical quality but (as a forensic and eschatological concept) a relationship to God. The one who believes *is* righteous, as the one acquitted by God's verdict.

The terms "sinners" and "justified" correspond to the contrast of "death" and "life." Throughout the entire passage the basic antithesis is characterized by various synonymous concepts. Even though "many" occurs here instead of "all men" as in verse 18, there is no change in meaning (see above).

This verse concludes the line of thought. The parallels between Adam and Christ have been fully developed through the detailed presentation of similarities and differences. When Paul begins to speak again of law in verses 20f, harking back to verses 13f where it was mentioned as something that stood between Adam and the time of Christ, he probably does so from apologetic or polemic motives in light of the Jewish position that life was mediated by the law. This makes doubly clear how closely 5:12–21 is related to the context of the ideas developed in 3:21—4:25. At the same time verse 20 adds a soteriological significance to the cosmological significance of the underlying gnostic myth in much the same way that the concepts of judgment and condemnation broke out of the mythological concepts, which were limited to "death" and "life."

VERSE 20. "But the law came in . . ." The law then is not the way to life but, as we saw already in verses 13f, the way to death. Its purpose was to multiply the trespass. But in God's plan this dreadful purpose was turned into a saving one. In the face of the effect of the trespass the superior power of grace came into play. "But whenever sin multiplied, there grace was even more abundant." At the basis of this statement is the realization that grace is for sinners only. Law, however, makes sin manifest; "It was added because of transgressions" (Gal. 3:19). It awakens slumbering sin (7:7–11) through which law produces death in order that it "might become sinful beyond measure" (7:13). Man's basic sin, the exulting which the Jew bases on the law, is to be defeated. There is grace only where there is no more exulting. "Then what becomes of our boasting? It is excluded" (3:27).

The cosmological sketch of the myth has become soteriological. The two periods of human history are not successive, as in the myth, but have an inner relationship. The first period, that of sin, prepares the way for the second, that of grace. We should not forget that Paul presents the inner relationship as existing only between two periods of human history, and is not thinking of the history of individuals. In the same way in Galatians 3:21–25 law is not "our custodian until Christ came" in the sense of bringing the individual into subjective despair, in which state he then awaits grace. Paul's thinking is rather of the objectively desperate situation of mankind, out of which man is led when he lays hold of grace

through faith, grace which is made a reality through
Christ.

Luther projected this soteriological idea into the history
of the individual when he said, "Ego ipse non semel
offensus sum usque ad profundum et abyssum despera-
tionis, ut optarem nunquam esse me creatum hominem,
antequam scirem, quam salutaris illa esset desperatio et
quam gratiae propinqua" (de servo arb. WA, Vol. XVIII,
p. 719). And in his lecture on Romans he says, "Unde
cum Dominus habeat nomen Salvatoris, adiutoris in
tribulationibus . . . qui noluerit pati, quantum in ipso est,
spoliat eum suis propriis titulis et nominibus. Sic enim
nullus erit ei homini Jhesus i.e. Salvator, quia non vult
esse damnatus; nullus eius Deus creator, quia non vult
esse nihil, cuius ille sit creator" (Schol. ed. Ficker II, pp.
135, 20ff).

VERSE 21. The final sentence describes how grace
abounded by using an expression, "as . . . so," that
brings out the basic idea of verses 12–21. "As sin reigned
through death" (this corresponds to the formulations in
vv. 14, 17) "so grace might also reign" (this corresponds
to v. 17). Here, however, the entity "grace" is named instead of the persons who receive the grace. By desig-
nating eternal life as the goal Paul identifies here at the
end of the chapter the theme, or problem, of 5:1–11,
12–21. By saying "through Jesus Christ our Lord" he
stresses again the saving event which has brought about
this renewal.

These two clauses do not correspond exactly to each
other either. It should run, "as law reigned through sin
to death," but Paul cannot say this. He would have to say
"sin through the law." Or it should run, "so also grace
reigned through life." But he cannot say this either, be-

cause he wants to mention righteousness, and it is impossible for him to say "through life to righteousness."

The final clause with ἵνα merely indicates the goal of the action. "So grace might also reign" does not say whether life is present or future. But when Paul states that the life in question is eternal he is probably thinking in terms of the future. Nevertheless, verses 12–21 show the believer's paradoxical situation. The future life is present in a concealed manner because Christ has come and because the believer's death, although still future, has been robbed of its significance as death. Justification (v. 16), or acquittal and life (v. 18), is present reality for those who are justified by faith (v. 1). It is not that believers will receive grace and the free gift of righteousness sometime in the future (v. 17), but that as believers they already receive them.

In contrast to verses 1–11, verses 12–21 show the paradoxical nature of the Christian situation by placing the emphasis, not on the transience of the present, but on the presence of the future.

How does Karl Barth interpret Romans 5:12–21? He interprets it in the same way he interprets 5:1–11 without paying attention to the context of the letter and the main statement of the question. Thus he does not see in 5:12–21 the description of the paradoxical Christian situation in which life is at the same time both present and future. He says rather that the theme of 5:12–21 is "the secret and the truth of *human nature* as such" (p. 41), man's being as such. While 5:1–11 spoke directly only of Christ and the one who believes in him, 5:12–21 speaks of man as man.

The connection between 5:12–21 and 5:1–11 is then

to be understood as follows. Because as men, as children and heirs of Adam, we already are within the kingdom of Christ the condition of believers is that which is described in verses 1–11 (pp. 42f). Thus Barth interprets the "therefore" of verse 12 as referring to the whole section 1–11. But he ignores the "as" (v. 12 is then probably not to be read as an *anakolouthon* but as a "kind of heading," p. 5) and then supplies a ὅτι which he regards as valid for the whole section 5:12–21. He explains that "because even while we were weak, sinful, godless, and enemies, while we were children and heirs of Adam, and thus even in the past from which we have come, we were not simply outside the realm of the truth of Jesus Christ, but were actually in a specific even though negative relation to his holy lordship," we exult through him in our hope (p. 5). "Properly understood, even our former existence outside of Christ was a real but still concealed existence in him. In view of this we boldly confess that we have peace with God . . ." (p. 6). Even in the midst of that first state not only the sin of Adam and its consequences, but "also the crucifixion of Christ, and through it our reconciliation, were already realities" (p. 17). "The same Jesus is also already present there" (p. 18).

I cannot find any of this in the text. Paul says nothing about adamic man standing under the lordship of Christ, but he presents the periods before and after Christ as total contrasts, the period of sin (and of law) and death, and the period of acquittal and life. Neither does he say that we exult as we look back to the period that is past, because Christ was already present there. He says nothing about our being able to discern in retrospect the ordinance of Christ's kingdom even in the world of Adam (p. 6).

While Paul contrasts the two modes of human existence,

Barth brings to the text the question of man's being as such: "what man's situation really and originally was" (p. 6), a question which in itself is quite proper and necessary. Even if Paul had not raised it the answer might still be contained implicitly in the text. But what is the answer which Barth feels he can draw from the text? That man's original nature is to be discovered, not in the picture of Adam, but in that of Christ (p. 6). Adam is to be interpreted in terms of Christ, not Christ in terms of Adam (p. 6). Christ's humanity is the key to the secret of man himself (p. 42)! "Verse 12 declares that in the same way that we were related to Adam we were originally truly related to Christ" (p. 7). All that is to be said about Adam and about us others has its truth in what is to be said about Christ and us others, "so that we are to understand Adam in terms of Christ and not Christ in terms of Adam" (p. 9; cf. p. 44). It only appears that Adam, like Christ, is the first, the chief of a race of men. "As men we are justified and saved in that Adam is not our head and we are not his members" (p. 10). It is this which "constitutes and contains our human nature" (p. 10). The one who appears to be the second is really the first, and the one who is apparently the first is really the second (p. 24). The truth is that Adam is "one among others" (p. 45).

But Paul knows nothing of all this. When he calls Adam the "type of the one who was to come" (v. 14) he says the exact opposite, just as in 1 Corinthians 15:45–47 he explicitly distinguishes between Adam and Christ as the first and the second man, and explicitly rejects the reverse order. Neither does Paul speak of human "nature," but of adamic man and Christian man. We can say, "Death was no more characteristic of primordial man than sin was" (p. 13), because of course sin and death came into the world through Adam. But Paul does not speculate about a primordial humanity of which Christ was the head, so that we could discover in the picture of Christ "what man's real and original condition was."

I believe I now understand how Barth came to this forced interpretation. I even believe that he is justified in saying that "what is Christian is, apart from all religiousness, secretly but unconditionally that which is common to mankind" (p. 43). But this cannot be based on the idea that Christ stands "above" as the "first," and Adam "beneath" as the "second" (p. 43). It is only meaningful if we say that human existence comes to its proper nature only as Christian existence, that is, in faith in God's grace as revealed in Christ. But according to Paul this grace is characterized by the fact that (as distinct from creation grace, if we may speak of such grace—something Paul does not do) it became real when the fulness of time had come (Gal. 4:4), and because in it the old passed away and something new came (2 Cor. 5:17). In addition, by it God's lordship was established, and before this time sinful adamic mankind had not been subject to his lordship. All this is obscured by Barth's exegesis.

Why is this so? He is apparently misled (unconsciously of course) by his thesis that we cannot say "law and gospel" but only "gospel and law." This is revealed in his exegesis of verse 20. He is right in saying that the trespasses are the "point of contact and origin" for grace (pp. 12f, 14, 18f). Yet the inner connection of sin and grace is not perceived unless the exulting is seen as the culmination, or as the real nature of sin. Consequently the soteriological significance of the law is missed. Barth interprets "to increase the trespass" as meaning "so that the trespass would not be concealed but remain visible" (p. 30). The heathen who did not have the law were spared from having sin "become so great, that is [*sic*!], so obvious in them also" (p. 31; cf. pp. 26ff). Barth solves the problem of "sin is not counted" (v. 13) by saying that men without the law "live according to their ideals and errors" (p. 27) because they sin unknowingly (p. 28). They have not really suffered from the division that runs through human existence! "They know how, by a little tragedy, to avoid confronting it if worse comes to worst" (p. 27). As if Paul were thinking of the culture of the heathen when he wrote "sin is not counted," and not rather of the period of time from Adam to Moses.

The meaning of "was even more abundant" in verse 20 is not seen as the supremacy over sin of grace *as grace,* but it is taken as having a threefold motivation. First, because Jesus as a Jew embodied the man who opposes God (p. 33, cf. p. 35). God himself "took man's place as sinner and as mortal" (see also p. 40). Second, because the Jews rejected Jesus, condemned him as a sinner, and had him put to death (pp. 33–36). Third, because Jesus' death is for all men, and thus the Romans were the ones who crucified him (pp. 37–40).

Finally, it is clear that Barth fails to recognize the mythological basis of the argument in 5:12–21. When he regards Adam not as the head of pre-Christian humanity but as "one among others" who, as such, represented mankind (p. 45), Adam has then basically become the idea of man. The myth in which Adam is the normative, primordial man has been "demythologized," but in a questionable manner. The manner in which Paul strives to turn the mythological cosmology into salvation history cannot be dealt with in this way.

Just as the figure of Adam becomes an idea, so also Christ seems to become an idea. When, according to Barth, Christ is absolutely the "true man," this then is not at all a concrete, historical man, but the idea of "true" man. Since according to Barth, the unity of man and mankind belongs to true human nature as one of its attributes, the result is that *"even the sinful man,* the only one we can know, mirrors in respect to this unity *the human nature of Christ,* and thus has not ceased to be true man nor to show us the picture of the true man" (p. 45). It is incomprehensible to me how anyone can find that in Romans 5.

NOTES

1. Since I am concerned with coming to grips with Barth, I do not intend to take up the interpretation of Romans 5 in recent literature, nor will I discuss the textual problems contained in some of the verses.

2. Translator's note: Since Bultmann gives his own translation of Romans 5, I have tried to reproduce it in English in a way that will show the particular points he is trying to make.

3. Translation ours. Page numbers refer to *Christ and Adam: Man and Humanity in Romans 5,* tr. by T. A. Small (Edinburgh: Oliver and Boyd, 1956).